DATE DUE

DEMCO 38-297

BEACON HILL PRESS
OF KANSAS CITY

Copyright 2010
by Beacon Hill Press of Kansas City

Printed in the United States of America

ISBN 978-0-8341-2488-2

Cover Design: Darlene Filley
Illustrator: Anni Matsick
Interior Design: Sharon Page

Editor: Donna Manning
Assistant Editor: Laura S. Lohberger

Note: This story is based on actual events that focus on ways the Church of the Nazarene reaches out to the troubled youth of East Timor (now officially recognized as Timor-Leste). It is part of the *Kidz Passport to Missions* curriculum.

10 9 8 7 6 5 4 3 2 1

DEDICATION

To my dear friends Warren and Janet Neal who, along with field missionary Acy Lodja, pioneered the work of the Church of the Nazarene in East Timor, now officially recognized as Timor-Leste.

our church LINKS missionaries during 2009 + '10

CONTENTS

1. Trouble Brewing — 7
2. The Other Side of the World — 12
3. The Plan — 18
4. Back in East Timor — 21
5. The Party Planners — 26
6. The Youth Center — 30
7. Changing Plans — 33
8. A New Discovery — 38
9. Surprise! — 43
10. Most Valuable Player — 48

1
TROUBLE BREWING

LaTeesha sat in the school cafeteria, craning her neck to look for Sidney. "She can't be lost," LaTeesha thought. "This is where we sat every day last year."

Still, it was the first day of a new school year. What if they had been wrong about having the same lunch time?

No way! LaTeesha could not imagine lunching all year long without her best friend. Gorgeous, bubbly Sidney made everything fun—even a boring day at school.

LaTeesha picked at her peanut butter and honey sandwich, suddenly not hungry. She looked toward the cafeteria door again. Finally, she saw Sidney heading her way. Her friend's long, blonde curls bounced with each step. LaTeesha patted her own tight black curls and remembered how Sidney always said she wanted to trade hair. LaTeesha thought she was crazy.

"Hey, LaTeesha," Sidney called, "who ya lookin' for?"

LaTeesha returned Sidney's wide smile. "My No. 1 lunch buddy," she answered. "I'd about given up hope."

Sidney plopped her trendy lunch cooler onto the table and sat down. She lowered her voice and leaned in. "Wait till you hear why I'm late. I have stratospherically [strat-tuh-SFIR-ik-awl-lee] good news."

"Stratospherically?" LaTeesha asked. Then she bit into her sandwich as she listened to her friend.

"Stratospherically is my new word," Sidney said. She unzipped her cooler and took out a pudding. Sidney always ate dessert first. Between bites, she explained, "The stratosphere is in outer space or something. We talked about it in science. Anyway, all the other good words are taken. I need my own phrase, you know? Cool people always have their own phrases."

LaTeesha grinned and shook her head. "You are so jaboozled [ja-BOO-zuhld]."

Sidney's big green eyes got even bigger. "So *what?*"

"Jaboozled," LaTeesha answered, totally straight-faced. "It's *my* new phrase, and it means goofy. Or dorky. Or . . ."

Sidney interrupted. "Got it."

"Are you sure? It could also mean . . ."

"That you aren't going to hear my news," Sidney said with a pout.

LaTeesha tried to look disappointed. "But I have to hear the news. I've never heard anything stratospheric before."

Sidney put her empty pudding container aside and got out a sandwich. "OK. After science class, I heard Josey tell Maria that she's not trying out for athletics!"

"Seriously?" LaTeesha asked. "If Josey doesn't try out, neither will any of her friends! That opens up at least five or six spots! More if word gets out. You're right, Sidney. This *is* stratospheric!" She hugged her friend. "We've got a way better chance of getting in now."

"Huh?" Sidney asked, pulling away. "If Josey's not going to be in athletics, what's the point?"

"The point is playing sports, going on all those cool trips, and winning trophies. Come on," LaTeesha said, "since when does Josey make our plans for us? We aren't in her group of friends."

"That's for sure." Sidney's gaze drifted longingly to the table where Josey and all the coolest kids in school sat. The group burst into laughter over something—probably an inside joke. "I don't know," Sidney continued. "Athletics isn't going to be the same this year. Everyone's trying out for choir instead."

"Everyone?"

"That's what Josey said."

LaTeesha rolled her eyes. "Sidney, we spent all last year totally bummed because we hadn't tried out for athletics. Then we spent all summer practicing for this year's tryouts. We've been dreaming about how much fun we'll have if we get in. I'm not going to let Josey ruin that. As long as you're in athletics with me, that's all I care about."

Just then, Josey's group strutted by on their way out of the cafeteria. They talked and laughed loudly while a cafeteria full of "ordinary" kids watched in awe.

LaTeesha could hardly believe it when Josey paused beside their table, smiling at Sidney.

"Hey, Sidney," she said in her high-pitched voice, "don't you have math next? Walk with us."

Sidney could not leave LaTeesha's side fast enough. "Sure, Josey!" she said quickly and too eagerly. She grabbed her cooler and stood up. "We'll talk later," she whispered to LaTeesha. "But don't count on me for athletics."

As LaTeesha watched her best friend work her way into the middle of the cool kids, the last bite of peanut butter and honey sandwich stuck in her throat. It would not go past the huge lump growing there. "Yeah," she thought. "Looks like I can't count on you for anything."

What had happened to her best friend and all their big plans? During the summer, she and Sidney met every weekday to stretch, run, and lift weights. They spent their allowances to buy volleyballs, basketballs, and track shoes. They practiced setting and spiking, dribbling, passing, and shooting.

Somewhere in the process, though, they actually transformed into "for real" athletes. Their workouts stopped feeling like torture and became fun. That was when LaTeesha knew their dream would come true—they would both make the Ozark Upper Elementary squad.

Now the hope inside of LaTeesha shriveled like a popped party balloon. Could snobby Josey really walk in and crush LaTeesha's dream in one millisecond?

"No!" LaTeesha decided. "I won't give up without a fight."

2

THE OTHER SIDE OF THE WORLD

Alfredo [al-FRAY-doh] stood with his eyes fixed on the small TV. It sat on a shelf over the shop's checkout stand blaring out words in English. He could not understand the language, but that did not matter. Alfredo considered the Los Angeles Lakers the world's greatest basketball team. And he did not need the announcers to tell him that No. 24 passed to No. 9, who arched it into the air for a three-pointer.

Alfredo cheered. His cheers turned into a painful cough, though, and he fought for breath. He hated the unknown illness that had invaded his life, making the simplest things hard for him.

Once Alfredo could breathe again, he had to scoot to the right because someone taller blocked his view. That happened a lot. For one thing, Alfredo was small for a 12-year-old, probably because he was sick all the time. For another thing, the men in town liked the Lakers too. And everyone knew Mr. Tim's shop had the best TV in that little corner of East Timor, their island country.

"Man, what are you doing?" someone whispered.

Alfredo glanced to his left and saw Richie, a kid he recognized from around town. "What does it look like I'm doing?" Alfredo asked. "I'm watching the game."

"Exactly," Richie said. "You should at least pretend you're shopping, man. Pick something up every once in a while. Check the price."

Alfredo did not bother to take his eyes from the screen this time. "Why?" he asked. "Mr. Tim knows I'm not going to buy anything." Mr. Tim's shop was like a home away from home to Alfredo. Actually, sometimes it was better than home.

"He'll yell at you and kick you out of his store," Richie said.

"He's not going to yell at me for . . ."

"Hey, Alfredo," yelled Mr. Tim, "this is a store, not a theater. Buy something or get out."

Richie gave Alfredo a look that said, "See?"

"Come on, Mr. Tim," Alfredo begged the owner, flashing his best smile. "You know I've got to watch my team."

Mr. Tim roared with laughter, and the wrinkles around his brown eyes deepened. "*Your* team? What do the big shot Lakers care about a skinny boy in East Timor? You're not even on the same side of the world."

Alfredo looked at the floor and mumbled, "At least I'm not out breaking windows and starting riots like . . ."

"Like who?" a voice behind him rumbled.

Alfredo recognized the voice of José. He was the leader of a local gang. José was 16. Unlike Alfredo, he was *not* small for his age. And unlike Alfredo, he *had* broken windows and started a few riots.

Alfredo gulped and looked behind him, searching José's angry eyes. "Like . . . um, I don't know," he stammered. "Not you, right?"

"Right!" José answered, sauntering out the door. "And don't forget it."

Alfredo blinked. Was that a bulge under José's T-shirt? Had he stolen something from Mr. Tim? What trouble would he cause next?

Some of the men in the shop must have been thinking the same things about José.

"That's a messed up kid," the tallest man said.

Another man shook his head. "What's wrong with teenagers today?"

"The same thing that's wrong with all of us," Mr. Tim answered. "Who isn't angry about what happened here back in . . ." He stopped and cleared his throat. "I won't go into it now. There are children present."

Alfredo sighed. When would he hear the whole story about their mysterious past? He stretched his full height. "Come on, Mr. Tim! Richie and I, we're 12 years old. Practically men. What's so bad that we can't hear it?"

The tall man said, "What's so bad?" He turned to the other men and spoke as if Alfredo could not hear him. "Look at him. He's OK, but what future does he have? His parents can't afford the school fee, so he roams the streets."

From the back of the store someone called, "He should get a job."

Mr. Tim snorted. "What kind of job could a sickly 12-year-old boy find? There aren't enough jobs for the men."

"Do your parents know where you are, Alfredo?" someone else asked.

Alfredo shrugged and acted as if it did not matter what these men thought of him. It was even harder to pretend it did not matter that his parents rarely checked on him. "They don't care as long as I don't make trouble."

"Of course not. Why should they care?" Mr. Tim complained, running a hand over his graying hair. "Just let Mr. Tim baby-sit all the kids in town, huh? I'm glad that Church of the Nazarene outfit is starting a youth center." He poked Alfredo on the shoulder good-naturedly. "Give you somewhere else to hang out. Get you out of my hair."

"Youth center?" That caught Alfredo's attention.

Mr. Tim smiled. "That's what I hear. You should look into it."

"Yeah," Alfredo agreed with a nod. "Right after the Lakers cream the Mavericks."

"What is it with you and basketball?" Mr. Tim asked.

Alfredo looked at the TV as he thought about it. He had loved basketball for as long as he could remember. He liked watching the way basketball players used their individual skills, yet played together as a team. He knew that basketball required skill and a sharp mind.

"Basketball probably takes his mind off his troubles," the tall man said. "Look at him. He's so caught up in the game that he doesn't even know you asked him a question."

Alfredo grinned. That's what he would let everyone think. But they were partly right about basketball. It did keep his mind off the problems he faced in East Timor and at home. His parents still believed in evil spirits and curses. They lived in fear of upsetting the spirits. It made life difficult at home.

Alfredo was not sure what to believe. He had seen the witch doctor use potions and cast spells. It was scary. His parents wanted the witch doctor to heal

Alfredo's cough. So far, Alfredo had managed to put off the visit. He did not know how much longer he could stall. He did not want to make the evil spirits angry. But he did not want to spend his life in fear of them either. He wished there was a better way to live.

"For now, basketball is about as good as it gets, especially a game like this!" Alfredo thought. The score was tied with 10 seconds to go! Then No. 2 for the Lakers passed the ball to No. 24 on the inside. No. 24 went in for a layup just as the buzzer sounded. The ball went through the hoop! The Lakers won by two!

Everyone in the shop cheered. Alfredo went crazy, cheering and coughing and cheering again.

"Poor Alfredo," the tall man said. "I can see that you love basketball. Too bad you'll never be able to play."

Alfredo stood up straighter. "Oh, I'll play someday," he said with confidence.

Mr. Tim put his arm around the small boy. "Sure, sure. Our little Alfredo here is going to play for the Lakers someday."

"Actually," Alfredo said, "I plan to play for East Timor. In the Olympics."

The store went silent as the men stared at him in shock. Then everyone in the store began to roar with laughter.

Suddenly, Alfredo felt his most cherished dream begin to die. He fought tears and threw his skinny shoulders back. "No," he thought, "I *will* play someday. I won't give up without a fight."

3
THE PLAN

LaTeesha rapped the "super-secret knock" on Sidney's window.

Tap. Tap-tap. Tap. Tap. Pause. *Tap. Tap.*

She saw the mini-blinds part and tried not to grin when one of Sidney's bright green eyes peeked out at her.

"Sidney will not win today," LaTeesha promised herself. "I'm going to stay angry no matter how cutesy, sorry, or pathetic Sidney acts."

She huffed an angry breath to prove how angry she was.

"Then what am I doing here?" she asked the sky.

"What are you doing here?" Sidney's voice answered from behind her. "You're here to see me, of course!"

LaTeesha turned to see Sidney flip her blonde curls over her shoulder just like Josey.

"And you're just in time," Sidney continued. "I've got stratospheric plans for your birthday party!"

LaTeesha shook her head. Sidney always struck from somewhere so out of the blue that she could not keep up. Or stay angry.

"I'm not having a birthday party," LaTeesha said.

Sidney spun around squealing, then grabbed LaTeesha in a hug. "You are now, and it's going to be the talk of the whole school!"

LaTeesha took a step back. "Oh, no you don't! You're not going to use my birthday to make yourself popular, Miss Sidney Anne Lewinski!"

Sidney's smile faded. "LaTeesha! I would never!"

"Oh, quit with the puppy-dog eyes," LaTeesha complained. "After our lunch today, how am I supposed to trust you? It looked like you were all about getting in with Josey."

Sidney's puppy-dog eyes lit up as she said. "Was that unreal? Did you see the whole crowd stop for me? Josey talked to me all the way to math class and saved me a seat next to her." Sidney faked a fainting spell, collapsing onto the grass.

Before she could stop herself, LaTeesha laughed at her friend's goofiness.

Sidney sat up and smiled her most contagious smile. "What in the stratosphere do you think that was all about, LaTeesha? Do you think Josey actually thinks I'm cool enough to hang with?"

LaTeesha plopped onto the grass beside her friend. "If she doesn't, she's not as awesome as everyone thinks. You've got it all, Sidney. You're beautiful, funny, and good at everything. Of course Josey would want to be your friend."

"You're sweet! But I don't know. I'm afraid to believe it."

"Me too," LaTeesha whispered.

"Huh?"

LaTeesha took a deep breath and tried to explain. "You know, I don't get the whole Josey thing, but you're my best friend in the universe, Sidney. So, if you want to be in Josey's crowd, well . . ." LaTeesha stopped to swallow. "I know I'm not gorgeous or super cool or anything, and so I understand why . . ."

"You are!" Sidney interrupted. "You are way gorgeous and beyond cool!"

LaTeesha tried to smile. "Then why don't you want to hang with me anymore?"

"LaTeesha! You thought I wanted to abandon you to join Josey's crowd?"

LaTeesha nodded.

"Oh, girl, no!" Sidney exclaimed. In one explosive motion, she jumped to her feet. She reached for LaTeesha's hands and jerked her up too.

"It's like you said," Sidney began. "For some strange reason, I am, apparently, already in. That means all we have to do now is get *you* in."

Alarm bells sounded inside LaTeesha's head. Sidney's plans often ended in disaster. She had to stop this one here and now. "Sidney, I don't . . ."

"It's no problem!" Sidney interrupted. "I've got it all figured out. I'm planning a party so over the top that no one who's anyone would dare miss it. It will be a massive success." Her eyes sparkled. "We're talking a whole new future for you, LaTeesha! Before you blow out this year's candles, you'll be one of the coolest kids who's ever walked the halls of Ozark Upper Elementary."

4
BACK IN EAST TIMOR

The evening after the Lakers game, Alfredo made his way back to Mr. Tim's store. He liked the shop owner, and he thought the owner liked him. He wanted to know why Mr. Tim laughed at his dream of playing basketball.

Something else drew him there too. He wanted to know what had happened in East Timor years ago that no one would talk about. Whatever it was must have been awful.

First things first, though. After Mr. Tim finished ringing up a customer, Alfredo quickly moved to his side and asked softly, "Why don't you believe I'll play basketball someday?"

Mr. Tim smiled, but his eyes looked sad. "There are a few problems with your plan," he said. "First of all, East Timor doesn't have an Olympic basketball team."

Alfredo glanced around the shop. He wished Mr. Tim would not talk so loud. There were other customers in the shop. Alfredo wanted Mr. Tim's advice, not theirs.

Too late.

"Our country will never have a basketball team," the tall man said, joining the conversation. "East Timor doesn't have money for training athletes."

"But we're sending someone to compete in the Olympic marathon. I heard it on the radio," said Alfredo.

The man chuckled. "What does a person need to train for a marathon? His own two feet and a stretch of road. That's all."

Mr. Tim sighed. "I saw on the news that our athletes are getting ready for the Para-Olympics. They're competing in wheelchair tennis with only one wheelchair. They take turns practicing."

"It wouldn't take much to train for basketball," Alfredo said.

The tall man raised his eyebrows. "A basketball would help. Do you have one?"

Alfredo looked down. "Well, no," he replied. "Not yet."

"And how would you ever get one?" Mr. Tim asked. His dark eyes were kind. "A basketball costs $20. Not one of us makes that in a month."

The tall man crossed his arms and looked down at Alfredo. "You've probably never even touched a basketball."

"Yes I have!" Alfredo cheered up as he recalled, "I went to visit my uncle once, in the city. And I played a game of basketball in a recreation center there." Alfredo covered his mouth while a fit of coughing shook his body. Catching his breath, he finished, "I was good too."

Mr. Tim exchanged worried looks with the other man. "How could you ever play ball, Alfredo? Just talking makes you cough."

"Oh, I haven't always had this cough," Alfredo explained. "But I'm getting used to it now. I won't let it slow me down. And East Timor *will* have an Olympic basketball team someday. They'll be heroes. You'll see."

The tall man stroked his chin thoughtfully. "Heroes? Hmm. Tim, remember 2000?"

Alfredo grinned. The man had invited Mr. Tim to tell one of his favorite stories.

"Well, now, let's see," Mr. Tim began, as everyone gathered around. "Before you can appreciate what happened at the 2000 Olympics, you have to know what happened in East Timor in 1999." The old man looked deeply into Alfredo's eyes. "You were . . . what? One-year-old then? You've probably never heard the whole story."

Alfredo did not move, did not even dare to breathe. Would he finally find out what horrible event had changed his country?

Mr. Tim sighed. "Maybe it's time we talk about it. Let's begin with a history lesson. Our country had been a colony of Portugal since 1520."

"You remember when the Portuguese first came, right, Mr. Tim?" someone in the back of the shop teased.

Mr. Tim laughed. "Go ahead, poke fun at my age. I'm proud of every one of these gray hairs."

"He's got so few of them left that he's probably named each one," another man said, making everyone laugh.

Mr. Tim smiled and continued. "In 1975, Portugal pulled out of our tiny country. Nine days after East Timor declared its independence, Indonesia invaded us. They ruled for the next 25 years."

"And people weren't happy about the way they ruled," one shopper commented.

Mr. Tim nodded. "Right. So when Indonesia offered us the chance to vote for independence, most people voted yes."

"And that's when it got real ugly," the tall man said.

"The Indonesian soldiers destroyed everything they could before leaving," said Mr. Tim. "Entire towns. Many people died. Wives, husbands, mothers, and fathers. Others fled from the country."

Everyone in the shop grew quiet. No one was grinning or teasing anyone now. Alfredo looked at their sad faces. Bits and pieces of other conversations he had heard made sense now. These people had lost family members, homes, and businesses.

Mr. Tim looked at Alfredo and added, "It's been 10 years, and we still haven't recovered."

Suddenly, Alfredo wished Mr. Tim had not told that part of the story. "Skip to the Olympics," he begged.

"I don't have to, Alfredo. I'm already there. You see, we didn't know it, but the rest of the world was learning about our struggle to become a free, independent nation. And they wanted us to succeed."

The old storekeeper looked beyond the people in his shop and continued, "I remember watching the 2000 Olympics on TV. They were held in Australia, just south of here. I'll never forget when our tiny delegation of four athletes walked into that massive Olympic arena in Sydney. The entire crowd stood and cheered."

"It did our hearts good to see that," the tall man added. "Strengthened us, somehow."

"Those athletes were totally overwhelmed," Mr. Tim continued. "They could hardly believe that all the cheering was for them. I've often wondered what it must have felt like."

Alfredo wondered too. He had seen that moment replayed on television many times, and he replayed it even more often in his mind. "Someday *I'm* going to find out," he determined. "Maybe East Timor doesn't have a basketball team. Maybe I don't have a basketball. Maybe I'm small for my age, and sick a lot. None of that matters."

Alfredo looked at the faces around him. He could hardly wait to prove them wrong. "No matter what I have to do to make it happen," he thought, "someday the world will cheer for *me*.

"Now, if I can just find a basketball . . ."

5
THE PARTY PLANNERS

LaTeesha sat in her favorite spot on the deck behind Sidney's house. She loved the view of the wooded hillside that led down to a wandering brook. Today, though, the peaceful scene did little to calm her.

She sighed and looked at her notebook, at the growing list of party supplies. She chewed on the end of her pen.

Sidney had spent the last half hour pacing the deck, telling LaTeesha what to add to their list. "We need one of those mirror balls that shoots little rainbow lights all over the room," she said. "That's, like, an instant party maker. And quit worrying. This party is going to rock!"

"Did I say I was worried?" LaTeesha asked, adding "mirror ball" to her list. That made four full pages of supplies!

Sidney pointed at her friend's pen. "You always chew your pens when you're nervous. You're going to chew right through the end of that one, and ink will squirt everywhere."

LaTeesha checked out the crushed end of the pen. "OK. Maybe I'm a little worried. For one thing, where are we going to put all this stuff? And all the people you want to invite? My living room isn't big enough."

"Right!" Sidney agreed. "We need to think bigger. Let's rent the school gym."

"With what money?" LaTeesha cried.

Sidney crossed her arms. "We'll have to use every penny we have, probably. But it will be worth it! This is your future we're talking about, LaTeesha."

"Why does that sound so familiar?" LaTeesha asked, rolling her eyes. "Maybe because it's the exact same argument you used this summer. We spent all our allowances on sports stuff, Sidney! You said our whole future depended on becoming athletes."

Sidney pouted. "I thought you had fun."

"I did!" LaTeesha exclaimed, tossing the notebook aside and taking her own turn at pacing the deck. "I had so much fun I couldn't wait to try out for athletics. But you've moved on, and now I'm supposed to forget all about sports and . . ." LaTeesha stopped. "I don't know if I can keep up with you."

Sidney put her arm around LaTeesha. "OK, maybe you don't have to."

"Huh?"

"It *is* your party. It's not fair for you to have to worry about it. You just show up and have the time of your life."

"And the money?" LaTeesha asked.

Sidney slapped her own forehead with her open palm. "Why didn't I think of this earlier? I'll tell my dad I'm throwing a surprise party for you. He'll help me out."

"But it's not exactly a surprise," LaTeesha said. "I know every detail."

Sidney huffed, "Well, I'll change the details, and then it will be a surprise. Do you want to be in Josey's crowd or not?"

"When did I ever say I wanted to be in Josey's crowd?" LaTeesha asked.

Sidney gave LaTeesha an affectionate slug on the arm. "Come on. Every girl dreams of being popular. Besides, I've seen the way you watch them."

A stab of guilt shot through LaTeesha, because she *did* watch the popular kids. She couldn't help it. Although she complained about them, LaTeesha had to admit she often wondered what it would be like to be one of the coolest of the cool.

"Besides, you want to be with me!" Sidney exclaimed.

"I'm becoming less and less sure about that," LaTeesha mumbled.

"Yeah, yeah," Sidney said, as she pushed LaTeesha toward the steps of the deck. "Now get out of here. I've got a surprise party to plan."

6
THE YOUTH CENTER

Alfredo left Mr. Tim's store and strolled down the street. At the corner, he dribbled an imaginary basketball and then pretended to shoot. He announced his own plays. "Alfredo shoots from the three-point line. And it's in! Three points for No. 46 puts East Timor up by 10!"

He grinned and continued to walk. He was not headed anywhere in particular—just wandering. Wasting time.

Alfredo's grin faded as he passed the school. He wished he were inside with the other kids. Standing still and closing his eyes, he remembered the sound—and the smell—of the white chalk on the blackboard. He could almost feel the smooth pages of a book in his hands and hear the sing-song voice of his teacher reading aloud.

How he loved school! Alfredo missed learning about far away places and things that happened long ago. He wanted to know more about geography, history, and science. He wanted to know more about everything.

A cough started deep within his chest and disturbed his daydream. He opened his eyes. At least his parents had been able to afford sending him to school through sixth grade. Plenty of kids he knew had not gotten that far.

He pretended to bounce a ball again as he jogged along. "And Alfredo dribbles down the lane. He goes in for the layup, and . . . it's good! No question, Alfredo is the team's most valuable player tonight!"

A man stepped out of the building Alfredo was passing. "You like basketball?" he asked.

Startled, Alfredo looked the man over. He did not look familiar. And what had the man been doing in that old, abandoned building?

"Couldn't help overhearing," the man explained with a grin. He held out his hand and offered Alfredo a firm handshake. "My name is Pastor Samuel, and I'm looking for some basketball players to break this place in." He motioned toward the building behind him. "It's the new Nazarene Youth Center. We're setting up a basketball court out back."

So it was true! Alfredo's heart began to pound with excitement. "Mr. Tim told me about this place," he said.

Pastor Samuel smiled. "Great! I'm glad news is spreading, because we want a big group of teens to hang out and play sports here. We're also going to offer English lessons."

"English lessons! That would be like going to school," Alfredo thought. Then he asked the dreaded question. "How much will the lessons cost?"

"They'll be free," Pastor Samuel answered. "No charge."

Alfredo did not even try to hide his excitement. "Where can I sign up?"

"Come on in. I'll get the list," Pastor Samuel said. "We can sign you up for Bible study, too, if you want."

Alfredo froze. Bible study? Uh-oh. His parents would never agree to that.

"Oh, um, I just remembered something," Alfredo stammered. "I better go now."

"But . . ."

The man's words faded as Alfredo jogged away. Away from the chance to learn again, away from the nice man and his basketball court.

Away from the chance to make his dream come true.

7
CHANGING PLANS

Wednesday morning, LaTeesha waited on the steps of the school and watched Sidney run toward her. Her friend's eyes sparkled as she waved a striped gift bag and announced, "Today's the day!"

"No, it's not," LaTeesha corrected, reaching for the bag. "My birthday isn't till Friday. Why did you bring my gift so early?"

Sidney snatched the bag away and hid it behind her back. "Who said anything about a gift? You greedy girl! This bag is full of invitations to a certain stratospherically cool party. I'm passing them out today."

"Oh!" LaTeesha's heart gave a skip. Sidney's big plan would soon be set in motion, and there would be no backing out. "Sidney, are you sure?" she asked. "What if the girls laugh at me for inviting them?"

"You aren't inviting them, silly. I am," Sidney reminded her. "It's a surprise party, remember?"

LaTeesha nodded. "Oh. Right. But . . . what if no one comes?"

Sidney smiled. "Don't worry. It's on a Friday night when nothing else is going on in Ozark. They'll come."

LaTeesha pictured a gym full of bored kids staring at her. Whispering about her. "What if they don't have fun?"

"Girl, don't you have any faith in me *at all?*" Sidney asked. "I know how to plan a party. Oh! There's Josey. Gotta go!"

LaTeesha watched her friend hurry down the steps toward Josey's group.

"If the plan really works," LaTeesha thought, "this time next week, Sidney won't have to walk away from *me* every time she wants to hang with Josey."

Oops! They were looking her way. LaTeesha turned around, pretending she had no idea they were talking about her. Like it did not matter what they were saying at the bottom of the steps, while she waited, breathless, at the top.

That evening, LaTeesha stood at the open door to her closet, trying to decide what to wear to church that night. Truthfully, she was not in the mood to go. She wanted to stay home and talk to Sidney on the phone. About the party. About the plan. About the way it was already working!

All day long, people who never looked her way had smiled at LaTeesha. Josey herself had spoken to LaTeesha while they stood in line to sign up for choir tryouts. LaTeesha could hardly believe it when the coolest girl in school invited her to sit at the popular kids' table during lunch!

But sitting there had not been as cool as LaTeesha expected it to be. The truth was that their jokes did not sound any funnier to her than the stuff she and Sidney joked about. And some of their conversations were not funny at all, especially when they made fun of classmates and teachers.

And signing up for choir, even with Josey, was difficult. Practices were scheduled at the same time as athletics. No way could she do both, and she hated giving up sports.

LaTeesha grabbed a blue striped T-shirt out of her closet. What had Sidney said? Choir with Josey's group would be more fun than athletics with a bunch of losers. And getting used to the conversation was part of the price they paid to fit in. Sidney thought they should just laugh at the jokes, not be so uptight. Everyone else went along with it. So how bad could it be, really?

LaTeesha pulled the shirt on and wondered if fitting in was worth it. Could she really change herself as easily as she changed clothes?

Should she?

LaTeesha perked up when she walked into church and saw the display table in the foyer. Missionaries! "That's right," she remembered, "our LINKS missionaries are here tonight!" She rushed to the table to look at the pictures and artifacts (objects used in the past) until it was time for the service to start.

Mr. Brown was the Nazarene Missions International president, and he sounded excited. "We are in for a treat tonight!" he told the congregation. "Most of you know that LINKS stands for 'Loving, Interested Nazarenes, Knowing and Sharing.' The LINKS program allows us to be 'linked' to specific missionaries for two years. During that time, we pray for them, write to them, and get to know them and their ministry. But LINKS missionaries don't always get to visit their churches. That's why we're so pleased to have Warren and Janet Neal with us tonight."

As the couple walked forward, LaTeesha compared them to their pictures that had been posted on the missions bulletin board for months. Janet was taller than LaTeesha had expected, but her brown curls and gentle expression looked the same. Warren looked like he was used to hiking and hard work. His mischievous grin and twinkling eyes made LaTeesha think he would be fun.

LaTeesha quickly got caught up in the missionaries' stories about East Timor. That's where their team is pioneering the work of the Church of the Nazarene.

LaTeesha did not know much about this tiny country on the other side of the world. She listened with interest as the Neals told them about the poverty and hopelessness in East Timor—especially among young people.

"We want these teens and children to know God has not forgotten them," Warren said. "We want them to know God loves them and has a plan for their future."

"Hmm. Does God have a plan for my future?" LaTeesha wondered. She pictured herself in the middle of the popular kids. "I wonder what God thinks of Sidney's plans for me."

LaTeesha turned her attention to Janet, who was now speaking. "We're excited about the youth centers our church is starting. They will provide a place for young people to gather and have fun. They will also provide sports equipment. There is no money for things like that in East Timor."

LaTeesha could not imagine being that poor. She thought of all the fun she and Sidney had over the summer, playing volleyball and basketball. And now they were not even going to use the equipment they had bought. If only there was some way to get all their stuff to the youth centers in East Timor! She wanted to do something to help.

All of a sudden it came to her. Maybe there was a way! She pulled out a pen and scratch paper and began listing ideas as they came to her—the party at the gym, the presents, the kids from school.

Sidney would not like it. Not one bit. But LaTeesha's heavy heart grew light. Could this new direction be part of God's plan for her?

She chewed on her pen frantically until the Neals finished. Then Mr. Brown spoke again, reminding the congregation how important it was to support their missionaries, Warren and Janet Neal.

That settled it.

After the closing prayer, LaTeesha dashed to the front to talk to the Neals about the big idea that just might change her life—and a few lives in East Timor too.

8
A NEW DISCOVERY

It was hard for Alfredo to stay away from the new youth center. He wanted so badly to play ball and learn English. One afternoon, he decided it would not hurt to walk by.

It did hurt, though. As he neared the center, Alfredo could hear the "thump, thump" of a ball hitting cement. It matched the "thump, thump" of his heart. The cheers and yells from the court called out to him as if they were invitations to join the game.

But his parents would not approve.

"What if I just watch?" he thought. "I shouldn't get in trouble for watching."

He crossed the street toward the building. A sign posted on the door caught his eye.

Sports Day Basketball Competition:
The Most Valuable Player
Wins a BASKETBALL!

Alfredo became so excited it threw him into a coughing fit.

A basketball? The winner would get his own basketball?

He looked to the right and to the left. There was no one around. Maybe he could sneak in and sign up without his parents knowing.

Alfredo paused. He hated to disobey his parents. He loved and respected them. But . . . a basketball?

For the moment, he forgot about his parents. He opened the door and walked inside. There were two long tables with chairs around them and a desk at the front of the room.

The man behind the desk looked familiar. He smiled and said, "Welcome! I am Pastor Samuel. How can I help you?"

Alfredo gulped. "I want to sign up for the contest."

Pastor Samuel pointed to a paper on his desk. "You can sign up here," he said. "The contest is next week."

Alfredo printed his name neatly and began to back toward the door. He needed to escape before any scary religious stuff happened.

"Don't you want to practice?" Pastor Samuel asked. "The guys are playing out back. I'm sure they would let you join them."

Alfredo looked out the back window and saw the boys shooting hoops. They were not the Lakers, but they were having fun. They were older than him, and pretty good. He *did* need to practice if he wanted to win the contest. After all, he had not touched a basketball for a long time.

Alfredo did not know what to do. He turned toward the front door, then the back window, then toward Pastor Samuel's smiling face. "OK," he said at last. "Will you ask if they'll let me play?"

The boys were glad for another player. Soon Alfredo found himself running up and down the court, passing, guarding, and blocking. It was even more fun than watching the Lakers on TV! And he held his own with the other boys. He only wished he did not have to stop every few plays to fight for breath. Maybe the men

at Mr. Tim's shop were right. Maybe his cough *would* keep him from becoming a great player.

Alfredo was glad when Pastor Samuel called, "Time for English lessons!"

The group filed eagerly into the building. As the other boys dropped into seats around the tables, Alfredo moved toward the door to leave.

"Won't you join us?" Pastor Samuel asked. "I'm a good teacher."

"I'm sure you are," Alfredo stammered, embarrassed. "And I would like to learn . . ." The word "English" was replaced by a cough so deep his eyes watered.

Pastor Samuel rushed to his side. "Sit down," he said. "I'll bring you a drink of water."

When the kind man returned with a cup of water, Alfredo accepted it gratefully.

"Stay long enough to catch your breath," Pastor Samuel encouraged. "And then, if my teaching bores you, you can leave."

The other boys laughed, and Alfredo joined in. When the lesson began, Alfredo drank in the instruction as eagerly as he gulped the water. He forgot about staying only to catch his breath, forgot about slipping out the door. He loved pronouncing strange new words like "friend" and "love." He liked the way English words tumbled over each other when Pastor Samuel read sentences from the big black book. He enjoyed the interesting stories about a teacher named Jesus.

Then Pastor Samuel closed the book and explained that Jesus was more than just a teacher. He was the Son of God who came to take away the sin of the world.

"Have you ever done something you knew was wrong?" Pastor Samuel asked.

Alfredo felt guilty. He did not have to think back very far. He had come to the center without his parents' permission, and that was wrong.

"Those wrongs separate you from God," Pastor Samuel explained. "But God loves you so much that He sent Jesus to take away your sins. If you choose to trust in Jesus, you can be forgiven."

Alfredo did not understand everything Pastor Samuel said, but deep inside he knew the words were true. Alfredo wanted God's forgiveness. And he wanted God's love more than anything, even more than he wanted to be a basketball star.

Alfredo realized this was the better way of life he had always wanted.

Pastor Samuel asked if anyone wanted this forgiveness. Alfredo stood quickly and walked to the front of the room. As Pastor Samuel prayed with him, an amazing thing happened. "I feel like I've had a bath on the inside!" he exclaimed.

The others gathered around him, shaking his hand and congratulating him. Alfredo had never felt so completely happy.

Alfredo did not notice when the front door to the center opened, and he did not hear the heavy footsteps that came his way. He did hear his father's angry voice, though. His harsh words brought the celebration to a sudden halt.

"Son, come with me immediately! You have an appointment with the witch doctor."

9
SURPRISE!

LaTeesha sighed. Once again she waited at the top of the school's steps, and again she spied Sidney rushing her way. But this time, Sidney was not happy, and it showed.

"You've ruined everything! Absolutely everything, LaTeesha!" Sidney growled as soon as she came close enough. "What in the stratosphere were you thinking?"

LaTeesha answered in an innocent voice. "It's supposed to be a surprise party, right? Well . . . surprise!"

"Not funny," Sidney said. "And I don't appreciate you telling everyone else before you told me. I worked hard planning the perfect party for you. It was going to make you popular. Change the course of your life! And now you go and turn it into some—some—charity event. What's that about?"

"Well, when I heard the missionaries talk . . ."

Sidney rolled her eyes. "Don't even start."

"But you wanted to know what . . ."

"What got into you. Right. What gave you the ignorant idea that the most popular kids in Ozark would want to spend a Friday night playing volleyball and basketball in the school gym?"

The bell rang, signaling the beginning of the school day. LaTeesha had never been so happy to hear it. She pushed through the open doors and headed for her locker, away from Sidney.

But Sidney followed her, talking nonstop. "As if turning your ultimate bash into some lame P.E. class wasn't enough, you had to mess with the gifts too! Come *on*. Do you even know what kind of haul you would have gotten from Josey's gang? Serious jewelry and iPods. Gift cards to stores where you could buy the right kind of clothes."

LaTeesha ignored Sidney while opening her locker.

"But, no," Sidney fumed. "You tell everyone to skip the gifts and bring donations for some youth center in a country no one has ever heard about."

Josey's high-pitched voice interrupted Sidney. "Isn't it amazing?"

LaTeesha turned from her locker to see Josey, not three feet away, smiling at them.

"Sorry to barge in," said Josey, "but I heard you mention the youth center, Sidney. And—wow—you told us LaTeesha was cool, but I had no idea. Giving up her *birthday* to help kids on the other side of the world? I love it! When she texted me her idea, I just melted. And volleyball and basketball? How fun is that?" She flashed one more brilliant smile before declaring, "I bought the cutest sweatsuit ever to wear to the party. So have your cameras ready!"

Then she was gone.

LaTeesha grinned at Sidney. "Need me to help scrape your chin off the floor, girl?"

Sidney stared down the hall, shocked. "What just happened?"

"I'm not sure," LaTeesha admitted. "But I decided to trust God with my future, Sidney. And something tells me He can handle it just fine."

Friday night after the basketball game, Sidney cornered LaTeesha. "I hate to admit it," she said, "but your party has been stratospherically successful."

"I know," LaTeesha agreed. "And guess what? Josey told me the reason she's doing choir this year is because she got kicked out of athletics for bad behavior. She still loves sports, though. That's why she couldn't wait to play tonight."

Sidney's eyes were huge with disbelief. "You mean all that stuff about athletics being lame was just . . ."

"Josey trying to sound cool." LaTeesha grinned.

"So now *I'm* stuck in choir for a year because *she* got in trouble?" Sidney asked.

LaTeesha shrugged. "Well, athletics tryouts are still open. I'm going to sign up Monday."

"Can I join you?"

"I wish you would," LaTeesha said, throwing an arm around Sidney as they headed for the volleyball court. "I'd be lost without my best buddy."

LaTeesha called her party friends together to assign teams. Just as she finished, Warren and Janet Neal arrived.

"Wait up, everyone," LaTeesha said. "These are the missionaries I told you about. They leave tomorrow to fly back to East Timor. I asked them to stop by tonight so we could give them our gifts."

Everyone sat on the gym floor. LaTeesha introduced the Neals, explaining, "When I told my friends about the youth center, they totally wanted to help. This is from all of us—over $300."

Warren and Janet wiped away tears as they accepted the envelope full of money. "Thanks so much for your generosity," Warren said. "This will make a huge difference for the young people in East Timor."

"There's one more thing," LaTeesha continued. "This summer, I bought my first basketball, and it's pretty special to me. But it might mean even more to a kid in East Timor. I know you don't have much room in your suitcase, so I deflated it." She pulled the flattened ball out of a gym bag and handed it to Janet. "Would you make sure someone really special gets this?"

10

MOST VALUABLE PLAYER

Back at the youth center, Pastor Samuel spoke first. "Are you sure you want to take your son to the witch doctor?"

Alfredo's father answered, "What else can I do?"

Alfredo knew he had to speak. "Father, I'm a Christian now. I don't want to be treated by someone who worships evil spirits."

"What?" his father bellowed. "You've abandoned the old ways?" He continued yelling at Alfredo so loudly that his wife came in.

"What's going on?" she asked. "Alfredo, hurry. The doctor is waiting!"

"I can't go to him, Mother," Alfredo said.

"Why?"

"He says he's become a Christian!" his father shouted.

Alfredo's mother threw her arms in the air and wailed. "A Christian? What's to become of him? He'll never get well!"

"I don't want to get well if I have to see a witch doctor," Alfredo said, wondering if he really meant it. Because now he knew if he did not get well, he would never be a basketball star.

Was he truly willing to give up his lifelong dream for God?

Yes, he believed he could trust God with his hopes and dreams . . . with his future.

As his parents continued arguing, Alfredo saw Pastor Samuel give the boys in the room a signal. Alfredo watched as the boys began dropping to their knees around the room. Their calm, pleading voices joined with his parents' angry voices.

The boys were praying!

As the prayers grew louder, Alfredo's parents grew quieter. Finally, Pastor Samuel asked, "Will you allow me to tell you about One more powerful than the witch doctor? I believe this One can heal your son."

Alfredo could hardly believe it when his father said, "All I want is for my son to be well. If you know someone who can help, please tell us."

Pastor Samuel told Alfredo's parents about God. Alfredo was overjoyed when they agreed to let the pastor pray for him.

Pastor Samuel placed his hands on Alfredo's head and quietly asked the Lord for healing. Alfredo thought he felt a sudden warmth rush through him, but then he wondered if he had imagined it.

"Now what?" his father asked afterward.

Pastor Samuel shrugged. "Now we wait and see. But I believe God has healed your son."

A week later, Alfredo showed up early for the sports day competition.

"How are you feeling?" Pastor Samuel asked.

Alfredo grabbed the pastor's hand and shook it enthusiastically. "I feel great! I'm so glad Jesus saved me."

Pastor Samuel laughed. "Good! But I meant your health. How is your cough?"

"I'm well, Pastor Samuel! God did heal me. I haven't coughed for a week!"

Pastor Samuel beamed. "Then get out on the court. Let's see you play!"

Alfredo began to warm-up. He loved running his hardest without stopping to get his breath. Now that he was healthy, he had a chance at winning!

Or did he? Alfredo began to wonder as more and more people showed up for the contest. Some of the guys must have been 20 years old! Even José, the local gang leader, was there. He and his friends were big and strong. Alfredo was small and not as capable on the court.

"I feel healthier," Alfredo told Pastor Samuel, "but I'm still a skinny 12-year-old. Think you could pray that I'd grow a few feet taller before we start?"

"You just play your best and leave the rest to God," Pastor Samuel answered, chuckling. He began assigning teams.

Alfredo was a bit frightened when he found himself on José's team. Still, he managed to talk his teammates into choosing "Lakers" for their name. It was a good move, because the men from Mr. Tim's shop were used to cheering for the Lakers. They came to watch and immediately adopted Alfredo's Lakers as the team to cheer for.

Alfredo wanted to make Mr. Tim and the others proud. "And maybe to show off a little," he admitted to his parents, who surprised him by coming to the youth center.

The competition was intense. Alfredo played his hardest and tried to leave the rest to God, as Pastor Samuel advised.

In the first game, Alfredo scored 12 points and blocked two shots. The Lakers won by 6, and Alfredo went crazy. Their second game was even closer. Alfredo only made a few baskets, but he got several good rebounds. José, who turned out to be a fabulous player, shot the winning goal with only seconds left in the game.

That put the Lakers in the final play-off game against the Tigers. It seemed that the whole village now crowded around the court to watch. It was almost like his dream of playing in the Olympics!

The game began, and the Tigers were amazing. The Lakers had to play harder than ever. The lead shifted back and forth—first the Tigers, then the Lakers, then the Tigers again.

The bigger guys stopped passing the ball to Alfredo, so he hardly got to shoot. He managed three baskets and several assists, but the game stayed close. As the clock wound down, Alfredo wondered how he could possibly be named MVP if no one let him get his hands on the ball.

"God, You know I want a basketball," he prayed, as he ran down the court during the final minute of the game. "And You know this contest is the only chance I have to get one." He spread his arms to guard his opponent. The game was tied, and he did not intend to let the Tigers score. "But even more, I want everyone to see how You have healed me, to bring You glory. Give me a chance to do something amazing, please!"

A Tiger passed the ball, and Alfredo jumped to grab it out of the air. The crowd roared as he headed for the Lakers' basket.

"Thanks, God!" he whispered.

Time seemed to slow as the crowd began the countdown. "10, 9, 8 . . ."

Alfredo counted on putting in the winning shot just as the buzzer sounded. But as he neared the goal, he was surprised to see that José was already there, waiting under the basket. José was the best player on the team. He never missed.

"Seven, 6, 5 . . ."

Alfredo had to do what was best for the Lakers.

"Four, 3, 2 . . ."

He passed to José, who went up for the shot.

"One."

The ball went in, and everyone went wild. The team rushed José while people in the crowd chanted his name.

Alfredo swallowed a lump in his throat as he watched the gang leader get the attention that could have been his. Still, his team had won. He knew he had done the right thing. But that did not help much when everyone gathered on the court for the award ceremony.

Pastor Samuel said, "With not one, but *two* game-winning baskets in the final seconds of today's games, is it any wonder that our Most Valuable Player award goes to José?"

José accepted the basketball and actually smiled at Pastor Samuel and the crowd. "Maybe this will be a new start for him," Alfredo thought. "I hope so."

"And now we have another presentation," Pastor Samuel continued. "Warren and Janet Neal are missionaries here. They have been to their home in the

United States and just returned yesterday. Warren, Janet, come speak to us."

Alfredo watched the couple walk to the front of the crowd. The woman smiled shyly while the man spoke.

"I enjoyed watching your competition," he said. "And I am pleased to hear from Pastor Samuel about the good things going on here. Our friends in America will be glad, as well. They are praying for you, and they asked us to bring a gift to the youth center." Warren reached into his pocket and pulled out an envelope. "Pastor Samuel, use this to buy whatever you need for this excellent ministry."

Pastor Samuel opened the envelope and looked at the check. Alfredo thought it must be a lot of money, because his eyes opened wide and then filled with tears.

After much clapping and cheering, the woman spoke. "We have one more presentation to make," Janet said. "A girl in the United States sent something back with us. It was special to her, and she asked us to find someone special to give it to. We've spoken to Pastor Samuel and watched today's games, and we know who is supposed to get this gift."

Pastor Samuel smiled broadly as he called, "Alfredo, come up here."

The crowd parted, making a path for Alfredo to walk up to the front. Mr. Tim began to cheer. The others joined in, and Alfredo could not stop smiling. When he reached the missionaries, he stared.

A basketball.

His own basketball.

"This ball is also a gift from God," Alfredo said. "He saved me and healed me. And now He has made my dream come true."

Once the cheering died down and the crowd started to break up, Alfredo asked Pastor Samuel a question. "Did you tell the Neals to give me the ball because you felt sorry for me?"

"Are you kidding?" Pastor Samuel said. "No one played any harder than you did. You were amazing!"

"But I didn't score the most points, or get many rebounds. Why did people cheer so much for me?"

Pastor Samuel stopped to consider. "Alfredo, have you heard the story about the team East Timor sent to the 2000 Olympics, and how the crowds cheered?"

Alfredo laughed. "Yeah, I've heard that story."

"Why do you think everyone in that arena stood and clapped for them?"

"Because they were such great athletes."

Pastor Samuel shook his head. "Son, they didn't win a single medal. But they represented a country that had been through horrible times and refused to give up. The people cheered because of what the athletes stood for. And today, you played well. But you won the prize because you played in a way that brought glory to God. That's why everyone cheered."

Alfredo walked home between his proud parents, dribbling his new ball on the hard-packed dirt road all the way. He thought about all the changes the past week had brought to his life, and he whispered a prayer of thanks to God. He knew that no matter what happened in East Timor, his future was secure.

Now, he could not wait to start practicing for the Olympics!

FACTS ABOUT EAST TIMOR

- In 1999, East Timor was torn apart by anti-independence terrorists who left hundreds dead and destroyed 70 percent of the small nation's economic systems. Hundreds of thousands of people fled the country. International troops came in to restore peace, but the road to recovery continues to be difficult.
- Despite the challenges their country faced, East Timor sent a delegation of four athletes to the 2000 Olympics in Sydney, Australia. Upon their entrance to the stadium, everyone stood and cheered. The East Timor team was completely overwhelmed by the warm reception.
- At the time of this writing, wheelchair-bound tennis players in East Timor are training for the Para-Olympics. They have only one wheelchair (a gift from someone in Australia) to use and must take turns practicing.
- More than 60 percent of the population of this country is 18 years of age or younger. Many young people cannot afford to attend school and are also without work. Some of them are upset about the state of their country and get involved in riots or violence.
- This is the setting the Church of the Nazarene has stepped into to bring the hope of Christ. One of the many ways the Church is reaching out is through youth centers that offer free English lessons, Bible studies, and sports events. Many young people have turned away from witchcraft and ancient nature worship and have come to Jesus. God has transformed them into vibrant Christians who witness to those around them.
- One such young man is the boy upon which this story is based. LaTeesha's character is also based on a young girl who asked her friends to bring gifts to her birthday party—not for her, but for children on the other side of the world. Her generous spirit allowed Nazarene missionaries to present a basketball to a boy who had prayed a long time for one.
- East Timor is now officially called Timor-Leste.